THAT
CHAMPIONSHIP
SEASON

JASON MILLER

THAT
CHAMPIONSHIP
SEASON

NEW YORK **ATHENEUM** 1972

FOR LINDA

WHO TAUGHT ME ABOUT GRACE.

INTRODUCTION

by Joseph Papp

WHILE I WAS considering the possibility of providing *That Championship Season* with an experimental production at the Public Theater, the playwright, Jason Miller, told me that a producer wanted to option the play for Broadway. I gave him my blessings.

During the next few months I had intermittent contact with Miller, who each time looked more intense and desperate than usual—which was considerable. It seemed the play was undergoing extensive rewriting to accommodate the views of a prominent director and the producer. Star names were being bandied about for the role of the Coach and Jason's eyes betrayed the look of a doomed prisoner hoping for the governor's reprieve. But still the prospects for the play's opening seemed bright.

A month or so later Jason appeared in the company of A. J. Antoon, the director. The pallbearers delivered the heartbreaking message—"Broadway producer drops *That Championship Season*." Would I consider doing the play at the Public Theater?

I had a lot of respect for the talents of both the young men before me. My feelings about the play, however, were mixed, which is not an unusual feeling for me when I am confronted by an unusual play. A good play is annoying. It defies any set views I have about what constitutes a good play and forces me to change my head around. That takes pain and a lot of effort.

What intrigued me most about Jason's play was its momentum, its sheer energy. I was worried, though, about its depth. The character of the Coach was fascinating—but wasn't he overdrawn? There were too many crises too close together—what was the central one? What about those overwritten speeches? But the characters were solid—fully drawn people. It was the kind of play I had been looking for. "Well, I just don't know." Two faces fell. "Why don't you get a few actors together and prepare a reading for me. I feel it's an actor's play and perhaps I can find the play through some living people."

As the days passed I observed occasional manifestations of the upcoming staged reading of *That Championship Season*. Once the mild A. J. is unleashed, he becomes a tyrant, relentless in pursuit. Names of actors were dropped in passing and I began to become aware of the casting concept. It was solid. I knew most of the actors being considered and they were good. There is no way of explaining why I began to look forward to that reading, why I felt it would be important, but I felt that way. The answer, however, was not that mysterious once I thought about it. It was the people involved: Jason, haunting the halls of the Public Theater; A. J. Antoon, a priest on a mission, with unmistakable faith in the play.

Those two to start with. And then one of my favorite
actors and dearest friends entered into the picture,
Charles Durning, whom I had found ten years ago
playing a cab driver in a basement where his talent
illuminated that dark cellar theater. I had taken him
by the shoulder and initiated this stocky, tough Irish-
man into the brotherhood of William Shakespeare.
For years he tackled all the great clowns of the Bard
with an earthiness and brilliance that endeared him
to the Festival audiences. Now Charlie was in the
picture and he loved the play. He wanted to act the
Mayor, George—a perfect role for him. Other fine
actors who had worked for the Festival over the
years, Walter McGinn and Michael McGuire, were
swept into the forthcoming reading and they, too,
fell in love with the play. It was undoubtedly an actor's play. The question still remained: was it an
audience play?

The day of the reading arrived. I had almost for-
gotten about it. In the Anspacher Theater Green
Room the actors, sitting on folding chairs, were trying to remember what they had rehearsed up until the
last minute. Jason, licking his lips, made himself very
small in a chair near his beautiful wife, Linda. I began to realize how important this moment was to
them. I prayed that I would like it. What will the
play sound like in the mouths of five good actors?

The reading confirmed my earlier likes and doubts.
But, *Championship* needed a lot of work and I de-
cided I couldn't commit myself to it right then. We
assembled the next day in my office. Both men sat

there looking at me as I broke out a bottle of good Scotch for numbing purposes. I think Jason's teeth were hurting, he kept his hand tight against his jaw. As for A. J., he was perspiring freely. "The play is still intriguing, but in the second act..." Thus it began. Three hours later I was still talking about the play and what had to be done and I just never got around to saying that I would not produce it. To my amazement, I found myself telling them to proceed immediately with the production.

Two months were spent in casting. Charlie Durning was fine for the role of George; Michael McGuire could play James to a turn; but Walter McGinn, who had participated in the reading as Tom, the alcoholic, was a question. Both A. J. and Jason thought he was too young or, rather, looked too young for the part. I thought he was fine, but made no effort to impose my view on the writing-directing team. Walter's initial enthusiasm for the play made the decision not to use him very difficult and nobody felt guiltier than Antoon.

This situation hung fire for a few days and I was visited by Walter McGinn. He insisted on knowing from me what I felt about his playing the role of Tom and I told him that I thought he could do it, but I also said that at this point I didn't want to force anybody down the throats of the playwright and the director. "Fight for the part, Walter," I instructed him, "and I'll support you." He thought that this was fair enough. The next thing I heard was that Walter had requested a reading in which he would deal with the age question. I wasn't there when it happened, but A. J., with a big smile on his face, came to me with the story. Walter had done a fantastic make-up job and had given a great reading and both he and Jason wanted him for the part. As it turned out, Walter McGinn's performance was a highlight in a play full of highlights.

The next two roles were the most difficult to cast, the Coach in particular. The role had the emotional scope of Lear and we played around with all the big names for a long time until Richard Dysart walked in to give a superb reading. Here was a dilemma: at the time we were in the midst of negotiating with a well-known TV star for the role. I informed Richard Dysart of the situation and asked him to give me twenty-four hours to reach a decision. Had I not felt the obligation to the TV star, I would have gone with Dysart immediately. He was a committed actor and had prepared his reading with great skill. He cared. We were under pressure. Dick Dysart had another offer, a very good one, dangling before him. What to do?

As good fortune would have it, Mr. TV carried the day for us. I was informed by his agent that he would consider considering the role under the following terms: 10% of that, 40% of this, and a billing over the title, plus a 60–40 split of the West African royalties. The only thing that he didn't ask was to share credit with the writer. I was relieved at the temerity of the demands, which I rejected joyfully, signed Richard Dysart, and moved on to the final casting—the role of Phil.

Paul Sorvino was one of four actors up for the role. They were all very good, but different. But when Paul sank his teeth into the part, something special happened. Here was my kind of actor—clear, precise, uncomplicated, but full of nuance. And so a fine company came into being.

Jason's head was in the script. There were still major problems in the text and one by one they were dealt with. Rehearsals were full of complications. A. J. had the job of whipping these diverse characters into shape and there were days when they all hated one another. Camps were formed, scapegoats created; the problem of the play was passed on to the personal relationships of the actors. There were many heavy scenes in my office which threatened the very existence of the play. There were days when they all turned on the director. Machiavellian maneuvers and tactics were employed—all manner of disruption—and each had to be dealt with firmly.

Through all of this Jason kept close to the play, where he belonged. I needed him to do the work, but the Broadway experience had taken its toll on Jason's confidence. I was worried until, one fine day, I made a point to Jason. He looked at me for a moment, swallowed hard, and said simply and directly, "I don't agree with you." I felt a smile forming somewhere around my heart. It was the moment I had hoped for and from then on there was no stopping him. He took over his play and claimed it. Every change he made was right; he knew his play and he began to see it work. In the final week of previews, Miller, at his full genius, whipped *That Championship Season* into its final shape, and it was a winner.

Championship has the smell of the theater about it. Good actors slip into their roles and Jason's sense of theater saturates the play. The work evokes the feeling of tradition, but in the real sense, the play is a modern work with its basic roots in America. Its simplicity is deceptive—but it is this simplicity translated into recognizable human form that gives the work its extraordinary power.

Unlike the middle-class suburban fare reflecting the economic status of its customers that is served up on Broadway, *That Championship Season* is essentially a workingman's play—a rarity in today's theater. The Public Theater is seeking the means and methods to reach larger audiences with greater diversity. Long before Jason Miller's play got to me, I had been looking for plays for broader audiences, plays that would be of interest and concern to all classes. *That Championship Season* is such a play. It is a "popular" work. It is a play for the people of America.

FIRST PERFORMANCE

May 2, 1972, Newman/Public Theater,
New York City

TOM DALEY	Walter McGinn
GEORGE SIKOWSKI	Charles Durning
JAMES DALEY	Michael McGuire
PHIL ROMANO	Paul Sorvino
COACH	Richard A. Dysart

PLACE : *The Coach's house, somewhere in the*
Lackawanna Valley.

CONTENTS

THAT
CHAMPIONSHIP
SEASON

ACT ONE

SET: *A large and expansive living room in a Gothic-Victorian tradition. The dominant mood of the room is nostalgia. Its furnishings are frayed, dusty; the cool and airless serenity of a museum fills the room. The furniture is a compilation of decades. Downstage left, a large mahogany table, over it a Tiffany lamp. A Stromberg-Carlson console upstage center. Large leather sofa and matching chairs are scattered around the room. Gun-racks, with shotguns, on both walls. Doilies on the sofa and chairs. Bookcase with glass doors upstage right, filled with leather-bound books, on top of it a small collection of silver trophies. Upstage center a large spiraling staircase winds up into the second floor. Overlarge and faded pictures of Teddy Roosevelt, John Kennedy, Senator Joseph McCarthy hang from the walls. Floor lamps flank the staircase. The wallpaper is faded and stained and the oriental rug covering the floor is worn and obviously in need of cleaning. An early-make, 1950ish, fourteen-inch television set, with rabbit ears, sits neglected in the corner. Upstage center is the main entrance, downstage left is the entrance to the kitchen. Soiled lace curtains cover the two*

*narrow upstage windows. On the dining table
sits a huge silver trophy.*

AT RISE: TOM DALEY *stands at the gun-
racks. He suddenly takes a shotgun from the
wall-rack.*

GEORGE
(Offstage)
Hey Tom, Scotch and water on the rocks?

TOM
(Holding gun)
No ice.

GEORGE
Scotch and water comin' up.

TOM
Bring in the bottle, no one's going to steal it. Hey
George, you know he keeps these guns loaded?

GEORGE
(Entering from kitchen)
Yeah, I know. Hey, put it down, I'm out of season!
Those guns have hair triggers.

TOM
I got the safety on.

GEORGE
Only my laundryman will know how scared I was.

(Pause)

You've been missed around here, Tom.

TOM

It's only been, what, a couple of years?

GEORGE

Three years, Tom. You've missed three reunions. Remember the time you put the wintergreen in my jock? I thought my balls were on fire. Those were the days, the good old days. I am sincerely more proud of winning that championship than I am of being mayor of this town. Do you believe that?

TOM

No.

GEORGE

Dirty bastard. I'll never forget you; you were a great guard. Brilliant playmaker.

TOM
(Deadpan)

You were a great guard too, George.

GEORGE

I mean it. Bottom of my heart. This is me talking, no politician. Tremendous ball-handler . . . I wonder what's keeping them.

TOM

They'll be here.

GEORGE
(Pops a pill)

Feenamint. Pressure is murderous. Tense. Get a little constipated now and then. Mostly now.

TOM

When do you start your campaign?

GEORGE

I campaign every day of my life. The real grind begins . . . one week.

TOM

I never thought Sharmen would end up a politician.

GEORGE

Everybody ends up a politician. I'll beat his ass. He
can't touch me in this town. Sharmawitz was his real
name. That was his family's original name. The
coach and me did some research on Mr. Sharmen.
The only thing a Jew changes more than his politics
is his name.

(Pause)

He wants this town. Yeah. He wants to take it away
from me.

TOM

Ready for another one, Your Honor?

GEORGE

James is going to be pissed at me if you're high when
he gets here.

TOM

Brother James wouldn't dare get pissed at you.

GEORGE

After the election I'm going to endorse him for superintendent of schools. Too valuable a man to waste his time being a junior high school principal.

TOM

That's patronage, George.

GEORGE

I know. Is there any other way?

TOM

What did they find when they opened him up?

GEORGE

Who, the coach? Nothing. An ulcerated stomach. That's all. He'll live forever. I love that man, as we all do. I owe my whole life, success to that man. He convinced me that I could be mayor of this town. He ran me. Do you know how goddam close that first election was? Any idea?

TOM

I don't remember.

GEORGE

Thirty-two votes. I beat Hannrin by thirty-two votes. I looked it up. Closest election in the history of Pennsylvania politics.

TOM

The Coach sent me a mass card when I was in the hospital. Mass card . . . I thought I was dead when I saw it.

GEORGE

How the hell long does it take to pick up fried chicken?

TOM

How's Marion? *Fat as usual.*

GEORGE

She's my conscience, for God's sake. My severest critic. She knows the political scene. . . . She's almost as sharp as I am.

(Pause)

You know, after the baby, she was . . . very depressed, not quite herself. She's coming around now, thank God.

TOM

That's good.

GEORGE

Hey, do you know what would make this reunion truly memorable?

TOM

Martin would come walking in that door.

GEORGE

Magic on the court, wasn't he?

TOM

Unbelievable.

GEORGE

Greatest high school basketball player I ever saw.

TOM

Unbelievable.
(Pouring)
Bless me, Father, for I have sinned.
(Drinks)

GEORGE

Make that the last, huh?

TOM

It's only six o'clock, George.

GEORGE

Six. It's nine. Where the hell have you been?

TOM

I drink on Pacific Coast time. That way I'm three hours behind everybody else.

GEORGE
(Seriously)
Do you have a drinking problem, Tom?

TOM

No. No problem. I get all the booze I want.

GEORGE

Look at you, you're underweight, restless, your memory's going, you forget people's names.

TOM

Almost forty, George.

GEORGE

Forty, yeah, it's like half-time.

TOM

Hey, I remembered somebody. I saw her standing by the library yesterday. Mary . . . what's-her-name.

GEORGE

Who?

TOM

The epileptic. Mary . . . you know, the one we banged in your garage. . . . We were freshmen or something.

GEORGE

I don't remember.

TOM

We humped her in your garage. She took fits or something.

GEORGE

Don't ever breathe a word. . . . She wasn't an epileptic. She was only retarded. Not a word. It could ruin me. She was raped here about two years ago. Scandal. Remember Mike Pollard?

TOM

No.

GEORGE

The guy with the glass eye. Yeah. He raped her in the cemetery. The one and only serious crime I had in four years. Dumb bastard. Where the hell is everybody? The coach loves to drive Phil's Caddie. That's why they're not here. Phil's got three cars now. Got a German car goes like a rocket. I cancel at least five speeding tickets for him a month. He's going out with this seventeen-year-old, believe that, up in Scranton. Had to take her to Philadelphia for an abortion.

TOM

He gave me a big hug and kiss.

GEORGE

Oh, he hugs and kisses everybody. Italians are like that. Can't keep their hands off you. Hey, what's air pollution? Five hundred Italian paratroopers.

TOM

What has an I.Q. of one hundred?

GEORGE

Poland. See, I'm Polish, but I don't mind that, don't mind at all. But Phil gets pissed. Moody bastard. You can never tell what he's thinking. But right now I'm waiting for Phil to kick in thirty thousand for my campaign.

TOM

Thirty thousand . . .

GEORGE

But in return, Phil keeps all the strip land he's leased from the city. Sharmen wants to break that lease. Mr. Sharmen is an ecology nut. The fashionable issue, right? If he gets elected mayor, you won't be able to piss in your toilet. And I'm going to whip Sharmen's ass all over this town. Not this town. Not here. This town is not going to change hands. I love this town, Tom, love the people. Sure we have problems, but if we pull together I can make it the greatest little city in the country. That's one of my campaign slogans. "Greatest Little City in the Country."

TOM

Original.

GEORGE

Yeah. We have some information for Phil that's going to knock him on his ass. He's holding back. He knows we need him. See, Phil's not bright, really. James has often said that about Phil. Marion went

up to see Phil last month about the contribution. He
stalled. She doesn't trust him either.
      (The MEN *enter.* JAMES *leads the way.* PHIL
      follows. JAMES *carries the beer.* PHIL *carries*
            two buckets of fried chicken)
Where'd you guys go for the beer, New Jersey?

JAMES

Phil wanted Schlitz. We had to go to Old Forge.

PHIL

Cop stopped us on the way back. But he—

JAMES

Speeding. It's a wonder he saw us at the speed we
were going.
      (Putting a six-pack on the bar)

PHIL

He recognized the Coach and me and ripped up the
ticket.

GEORGE

Where's the Coach?

PHIL

He's parking the car.
      (Grabs GEORGE*)*

GEORGE

I'd better put this in the oven.

PHIL

Who do you love, George?
(GEORGE *goes into kitchen with chicken,* PHIL
follows with beer)

JAMES
(Entering. To TOM*)*
How're you doin'? Stay sober. I may need you to-
night.

TOM

When the shit hits the fan I'll be right behind you.

JAMES

You can handle this stuff in moderation. You can
handle anything in moderation.
(To GEORGE, *who is entering)*
He didn't say a word. Evaded the subject completely.

GEORGE

Didn't he even mention . . . ?
(Phil enters with beer in hand)

PHIL

Chicken's in the oven.

GEORGE

Hey, Phil, did you bring along your dirty movies?
He's got pornographic movies, the dirty bastard. I
love him. I should arrest him.

PHIL

Arrest me? I rent them from your brother-in-law, the chief of police.

(*To* TOM)

The police department is a library for stag films.

GEORGE

He sells what he's confiscated. Isn't free enterprise something else?

PHIL

How do you think I raised the money for the Little League Fund? Rented the V.F.W., charged five bucks a head, and showed *Olga's Massage Parlor* and selected shorts.

GEORGE

Rin Tin Tin Gets In.

JAMES

Incredible. I couldn't believe my eyes.

PHIL

Who are you kidding. You bought a German shepherd the next day.

(*Loud whistle on porch*)

(COACH *comes in dressed in a brown suit, 1940 cut. White shirt. Tie. Gold watch chain. Huge man. Old Testament temperament. A superb actor. A man of immense and powerful contradictions*)

COACH

All right. Line it up. Shape it. Twenty laps around the room. Too much fat in the ass around here. I want my boys lean and mean.
(Great laughter)
A voice from the past boys, the old gunner can still bray with the best.
(Pouring whiskey)
Hit those boards hard, Romano . . . And you, Sikowski, don't just stand there with your finger up you know where, move! . . . And you, Daley, have a drink. . . .
(Laughs)
And you big Daley [JAMES], hustle some of this whiskey into you. Imported. Jamison. Boil your brains, this stuff!

GEORGE

You haven't changed in twenty years.

COACH

I haven't changed in sixty years. I can take the four of you around the court till you drop, run you into the ground.
(Proudly)
Even one eighty-five. Weighed that in 1940.
(Gets down and does ten quick push-ups)
And that's after having my belly cut open, twenty stitches.
(Opens shirt)
Look at that sonofabitch. Belly looks like a baseball.

JAMES

What's the secret?

COACH

"Walk softly and carry a big stick."
                (Pause. Great joy, shy almost)
Oh, Christ, boys, Christ, it's so good . . . the joy
in my heart to feel you around me again,
                (He pats, feels, whacks them all)
together again, can't find words to say it. . . . Magnificent! My boys standing around me again! A toast
to the 1952 Pennsylvania State High School Basketball Champions!
                (They drink)
You were a legend in your time, boys, a legend.
Never forget that, never.

GEORGE

We owe it all to you, Coach.
                (MEN *ad lib agreement*)

COACH

I used to tell people you boys were like a fine watch.
My very expensive and fine watch that kept perfect
time. You froze the ball against Tech for three minutes. Fantastic. Stay in shape. Lean and mean.
You're in your thirties and that's the heart-attack
season, boys. Most important muscle in your body,
boys . . . the heart . . . keep it in shape, work it
out!

GEORGE

Bought one of those exercise bikes. Keeps the stomach flat.

PHIL

But your ass is still down around your knees.

GEORGE

That's it, start on me, the old scapegoat.

TOM

You love it.

GEORGE

Yeah.

COACH

Drink up, boys, put it away, night's young! Take off your jackets, relax.

GEORGE

Chicken is in the stove.

COACH

You're working on your third chin yourself, Phil.

PHIL

I'm an executive.

COACH

James, you're starting to sag a little too, you look tired.

JAMES

I haven't been sleeping well, Coach.

COACH

Why?

JAMES

My teeth.

COACH

What's the matter?

JAMES

They're gone.

COACH

Gone.

JAMES
(Embarrassed)

They took them out last month.

COACH

You got plates?

JAMES

Yeah.

COACH

Let's see. Open your mouth. Uh-uh. Good job. They
look almost real.
(PHIL *laughs*)
Never had enough Vitamin C in your diet!

JAMES
(Half-smile)

Try feeding five kids.

COACH

You didn't feed them your teeth, did you? You need
iron in your blood. . . .
(Opens mouth)
I got twenty-seven originals.
(MEN *laugh)*

JAMES

Actually they've recently completed studies proving
that nerves can cause severe damage to teeth.

COACH

Really! Maybe you should have gotten your nerves
out!
(Laugh)
Have another shot and relax, James.

COACH

Better put that chicken on low, George. Tom, . . .
(Hugs him; they touch glasses and drink)
I'm so goddam happy, so grateful you're back with
us again. Doesn't he look wonderful, boys?

TOM
(Pouring)

Nothing keeps the old gunner down, either.

COACH

You were a thing of rare . . . beauty, boys. Life is

a game and I'm proud to say I played it with the best. We were one flesh twenty years ago; never forget that as long as you live!

(Pause)

Ten seconds left on that clock . . . we were down by one point . . . remember . . . unbelievable!

GEORGE
(Quiet intensity)

I passed inbounds to Tom.

TOM

I brought the ball up.

PHIL

Passed to me in the corner.

COACH
(Urgent)

Six seconds left!

PHIL

I hit James coming . . .

JAMES

Across the court and I saw . . .

COACH

Three seconds left!

JAMES

Martin at the foul line . . .

GEORGE

Martin caught the ball in mid-air . . . he went up . . .

JAMES

Up . . .

COACH

One second . . .

GEORGE
(Jumping up)

Yes!

COACH

State Champions! They said we couldn't do it, boys. We beat a school three times our size. We beat them in Philadelphia. We performed the impossible, boys, never forget that, never. Jesus, remember they had an eight-foot nigger, jumped like a kangaroo.
(Proudly)
There's the trophy, boys. Fast, Jesus, fast, you were a flash of legs . . . gone, like lightning!

GEORGE

Martin was a pressure ballplayer.

COACH

He thrived on it . . . loved it.

JAMES

He had a great eye.

COACH

Priceless.

GEORGE

The perfect ballplayer.

COACH

Not a flaw. He made it all go . . . magnificent
talent!
(Pause. Quietly)
Yeah. Not a word in twenty years. Let's say a little
prayer for him, boys, a prayer that he's safe and
happy and still a champion.
*(They lay their hands together. Moment of
silence)*
We never had a losing season, boys; there's not
many that can say that. . . .

GEORGE
(Testing)
Sharmen won't be able to say that after next month,
will he, Coach?

COACH

He'll see politics played like he's never seen it played
before. We'll run him off the court, that little mockie
is going to think . . . He's trying to ruin Phil. Put
Phil out of business.

PHIL

I strip-mine coal and the sonofabitch makes me out
to look like a criminal.

COACH

Phil is one of the most respected businessmen in the state and this . . . Sharmawitz is trying to ruin his good name. Cop ripped up that speeding ticket tonight when he recognized Phil.

PHIL

He knew you too, Coach.

GEORGE

He attacked me.

TOM

Who, the cop?

GEORGE

Sharmen. I'm not prejudiced. Live and let live. But that Jew attacked me, the mayor of the town, attacked me in print!

TOM

He's running against you, for Christ—

GEORGE

There's still such a thing as respect for the office! He said I wasn't smart enough to be corrupt . . . in the papers. Do you believe that?

TOM

Yes . . .

COACH

Fashion politics; he's running on all the headlines.

PHIL

The women love him. Looks like Robert Goulet.

GEORGE

You can't beat experience. He said under my term this town took five giant steps into the past. Believe that? I gave this town four memorable years!

COACH

And you'll give us four more! Like old T.R. said, Teddy was fond of sayin', "Never settle for less than success." And, boys, they carved that man's face into a mountain. They don't make Teddys any more, a man among men, a giant. Took Panama from the spics, boys, just walked in and took her.

TOM

I'll drink to that . . . feat.

COACH

And I'm proud to see all of you climbing to the top of your professions, politics, business . . . education . . . travel.

JAMES

And there's only one man I know who's responsible for it and he's sitting right across from me.

COACH

No, not me. You did it yourselves. Best advice I gave
you . . . get yourselves a name, remember? Listen
up, Phil, your Little League team lost its third in a
row, I hear.

PHIL
(Laughing)
Lost my best pitcher and my center fielder.

COACH

Injured?

PHIL

They go to camp in June.

JAMES

Use my James. He can play center field.

PHIL

He can't hit a curve.

JAMES

He's only twelve years old, for God's sake.

PHIL

Work with him. He needs a lot of work.

JAMES

You're the coach, not me. He learns fast.

PHIL

I don't think he's interested if you want the
truth. . . .

JAMES

He's a gifted child.

COACH

Very smart.

JAMES

He has an I.Q. of one fifty-five.

PHIL

That's about two points higher than his batting average.

TOM

Maybe you could trade him, Phil. . . .

JAMES

It's not funny. The boy is first-team material. His
self-esteem is being damaged, not playing, sitting on
the bench.

COACH

George, get me a beer.

(He does)

JAMES

He's just not your ordinary kid.

PHIL

He doesn't like the game. . . .

JAMES

Not sitting on the end of the bench.

TOM

James, he told me he didn't want to play ball.

JAMES

I want him to play.

TOM

He knows that but he doesn't share your enthusiasm.

JAMES

He's in that difficult age now. Avoids me. Keeps to
himself.
(Pause)
I think he's masturbating.

TOM

On the bench!

JAMES

You're ridiculous!

COACH

Did you say anything?

JAMES

What can I say? I certainly am not going to tell him

those old horror stories. My father told us we'd go
insane. Grow hair on the palm of our hands.

COACH
You kept it in your pants when you played for me.

JAMES
He'll do it, he will. I'll see to it. He's the cream of
the crop, that boy. . . .

COACH
You keep him playing. You quit on the field you'll
quit in life. It's on the playing fields the wars are
won.

JAMES
He's a good boy, a respectful boy.

COACH
He couldn't be anything else, being your son. You
were the perfect son. You took care of your father.

JAMES
(Simply)
Someone had to do it.

COACH
There's no respect, no personal sacrifice, not today.
There's not many who'd have made the sacrifice you
did, James.

GEORGE

There's a decline of respect, an absolute decline. . . .

COACH

You see, there's no discipline, George.

GEORGE

The high school newspaper had a picture of a pig with Phil's name under it, believe that? Sharmen was behind that.

PHIL

Number one threat to the environment. They called me that. The stupid bastards don't realize you can't kill a mountain. Mountains grow back. . . .

GEORGE
(Mollifying)

I fixed it up, Phil. Don't forget that, don't worry about it.

PHIL

What, me worry? I could buy and sell those little bastards a hundred times. I got a shovel working for me now, looks like a dinosaur, right?

GEORGE

I can still get you an apology in print.

PHIL

I don't need it.

GEORGE

I called the principal and gave him hell, chewed his ass out.

TOM
(Going upstairs)

That's it! I've got it! That's your campaign poster, George. A picture of you on your knees, salivating. Captain—"I'll chew the ass out of unemployment."

GEORGE
(Laughing)

I want him. Hire that man.

TOM

Where's the john?

COACH

Where it always was.
(Laughs; TOM *exits)*

JAMES

He was very sick. I think it's affected his memory. He's getting back in shape.

COACH

Nothing's going to beat that boy. He's comin' along, comin' along. . . . Let's put him to work on your campaign. Write press releases, speeches. . . .

GEORGE

My speech writer.

JAMES

I'd love it, but he's leaving. He bought his ticket today, he said.

COACH

Why?

JAMES

That's him, here today, gone tomorrow. Says he wants to leave by Sunday.

COACH

I'll talk to him. Give me an hour with him. Talk some sense into that boy's head.

GEORGE

We could use him.

PHIL

We need something . . . a miracle or something.

GEORGE

What does that mean, Phil?

PHIL

It means we've got problems.

GEORGE

Who?

PHIL

You. Us.

GEORGE

I've got a great record . . . wonderful. This town
loves me.

(Laughs)

Tell him how popular I am, Coach.

COACH
(Pause)

Let's hear Phil. . . . Don't overestimate your
strength, George.

GEORGE

What?

COACH   .

What I mean to say is never underestimate your op-
ponent.

GEORGE
(Pressing)

I'm putting this town back on its feet again!

PHIL

Not with your taxes. A four percent increase in
property tax. You're lucky you weren't hung!

GEORGE

We were broke. The city was broke when I took
over. We needed money, operating capital.

PHIL

No work around, no money, taxes raised every year.

People . . . want . . . change. Look, it's a small town . . . forty, maybe—

JAMES

Fifty-four thousand is our total population. There is unemployment but studies have shown that our unemployment is below the average.

GEORGE

You can't tell me that the workingman's not behind me.

PHIL

Workingman. The ammunition plant closes in September.

GEORGE

Phil, I didn't end the war.

PHIL

Look, I'm only reciting history. We had a garbage strike here lasted for five weeks. City smelled like a whorehouse.

JAMES

George has given this city the finest playground facilities in the state. I mean the program is considered a model by other cities.

COACH

That's a fact.

PHIL

And Sharmen has IBM ready to come in here tomorrow.

COACH

You bring those gigantic companies in here and in five years the briefcases will run this town.

GEORGE

I'm popular. Extremely popular. Wasn't there five thousand people cheering in the rain when I opened the zoo?

PHIL

They were waiting to see the new elephant—

GEORGE

But I bought the goddam thing.

PHIL

And it died in a month, George. It lived for one month only.

GEORGE

I'm the mayor, not a vet. How was I to know it was sick?

JAMES

I think what Phil is trying to say is that this—

PHIL

I know what I'm trying to say, James. It took you a month to bury the goddam thing.

GEORGE

Ten days, not a month, ten days.

PHIL

You could have burned the thing in a day.

GEORGE

You can't burn dead elephants. It's against the health laws. Don't you people know that?

COACH
(Pause)
The goddam thing drew more people dead than alive.

JAMES

Well, we got rid of it.

PHIL

You advised him, James.

GEORGE

Yes, I finally had to throw the damn thing down a mine shaft. Goddam city council made me look foolish.

PHIL

Had to rent a crane. Another five hundred bucks. The newspapers weren't kind, George.

GEORGE

They came around after I called them up and chewed some ass.

PHIL

They called you Sabu for a month. It hurt your image.

(TOM *enters*)

GEORGE

And I have a fantastic image in this town. If the city council was behind me, I'd get action and you know it. How can I work with a divided council, the bastards—

COACH

Trash it out, boys, trash it out. Have another drink, George.

GEORGE

No riots on my streets, no niggers burning down my town . . .

PHIL

The last nigger here was Joe Louis and he was passing through.

GEORGE

No radicals here, hippies. One rape in four years. One felony. My streets are safe any hour, day, night.

JAMES

We are not even certain she was raped.

COACH

Who?

GEORGE

The girl that Mike Pollard raped . . . he had a glass eye, you remember. . . .

JAMES

She claimed he assaulted her . . . forced perverted acts. Said he performed cunnilingus on her.

COACH

Cunny-what?

JAMES

Oral sex. The male performing an oral act on the woman.

COACH

Oh yes, oh yeah. Jesus, that's a fancy name for it.
(Laughs)

PHIL

If that's a perversion I should be in a cage.

COACH

Let's not get away from the subject, boys, we are on a very serious subject. I'm talking about dissension, boys, I can sense dissension in this room.
(To TOM)
Dissension is destroying this country, tearing it apart. You're George's speech writer. This country is hurting, boys, hurting, so let's pull together here . . . teamwork!

JAMES

Dangerous times all over.

COACH

We are killing off, murdering the best among us, gunning down the best we have! . . . Kennedy . . . killed by his own . . . such a waste.

JAMES

We don't take care of our own anymore. Bobby Kennedy, too.

COACH

They killed McCarthy, boys, his own kind killed a great American. Looked under the rock and found the place infested with communists. Joe McCarthy. Turned his name into a dirty word. They kill the good ones, they kill them quick.

JAMES

It's been a tough decade.

COACH

It never changes. Father Coughlin . . . you're too young to remember . . . he told the truth about certain people, on the radio, international bankers, Jews, fellow travelers, and they muzzled him, a priest of God telling the truth and they put him away, exiled him. And that's a fact, boys. We are the country, boys, never forget that, never. Thousands of cities like ours; we fire the furnace, keep it

all going round, indispensable! But no dissension, none, stick together. We stick together,
> (*Grabs* GEORGE, *dances*)

and "There'll be a hot time in the old town" come election night.

GEORGE
(Singing)

"A hot time in the old town tonight." Come on, you guys, sing . . . sing. This is a reunion, remember?

PHIL
(Clapping)

You sing, George.

GEORGE

Get the women, Phil, I think he's getting horny.
> (MEN *ad lib remarks*)

COACH

I'll run them into the ground.
> (*The* COACH *stands frozen with pain*)

GEORGE

What's the matter? Are you all right?

COACH

Bring me that chair.

JAMES

Can you move? Take a drink.

PHIL

What is it?

COACH
(Doesn't sit)

My stomach.

PHIL

Do you have pills?

COACH

It comes and goes. I overdid it. Adhesions, that's all
it is. The incision is healing.

GEORGE

What can we do?

COACH
(Trying to joke)

Give me a hand upstairs.

GEORGE

I've got him.

COACH

I'll put on that goddam girdle they gave me. It gives
me a rash in this weather.
     (On landing, as GEORGE *helps him upstairs)*
It's nothing serious, it's only a healing pain, I'll be
down in a few minutes.
          (Pause. COACH *and* GEORGE *exit)*

PHIL

He didn't look good to me.

JAMES
(Uncertain)

All that dancing around. He gets like a boy. He overdid it.

PHIL

He looks yellow or something.

TOM

He's sick.

JAMES

He overdid it.

GEORGE
(On landing)

He's all right. He's mixing something. Kelp. Says it's
an organic painkiller. I'll stay with him.
(Goes back to COACH)

JAMES

Okay.

PHIL

Kelp?

JAMES

Yeah. He doesn't believe in painkillers. No pills.

PHIL

He is going to get assholed by Sharmen.

JAMES

Shhh. Why are you so down on him?

PHIL

Because he's a loser. Four years ago he beat that old
alcoholic we had by thirty-two votes, remember. Five
recounts! You know it and I know it.

JAMES

Is that the only reason you're against him now?

PHIL

Isn't that enough?

JAMES
(Pause)

I thought it might be because you're having an affair
with his wife.

TOM

Christ. Not now, James.

JAMES

I'll handle this.

PHIL

Who told you?

JAMES

It could easily become common knowledge.

PHIL
(Almost pleased)

It's a rumor.

JAMES

Don't deny it, Phil.

PHIL

She never got over me since high school.

TOM

Old Marion. I hope she improved with age.

JAMES

You keep quiet, understand!

TOM

Humping Marion was part of the curriculum.

PHIL

Not when she went with me.

JAMES

Don't get involved with her, Phil, she's sick, she's unstable.

PHIL

She was a great girl till she married that asshole.

JAMES

That asshole stands between you and a complete
business disaster.

PHIL
(Shouting)
I know that, you think I don't know that!

JAMES

You need him as much as he needs you.

PHIL

Sharmen needs contributions too.

JAMES
(Stunned)
Jesus, you'd do that to us. You'd jump to Sharmen.

PHIL

An investment. Politics is just another way of makin'
money. Sharmen is no different than any other politician.

JAMES

I don't care what you do with your private life, but
when it endangers—

PHIL

You're in it for what you can get, a piece of the
action, don't shit me.

JAMES

He's all we have right now.

PHIL

And he's not enough!
(Pause)

JAMES

There is another alternative. My career is politics, Phil. I'm a political animal. I hoped to run, as you know, for school superintendent next year with George's endorsement.
(Pause)
I want you to realize that this is ahead of my time-schedule, and I only offer my candidacy because we seem to be faced with an insoluble crisis.

PHIL
(Pause)
You're not serious.

JAMES

Run me, Phil. I can carry this town.

PHIL
(Stunned)
Why don't you have a drink, James?

JAMES

Someone has to challenge Sharmen's charisma.

PHIL

I'll have one with you.

JAMES

My reputation is spotless. I'm a respected public of-
ficial. Known all over town. George could be convinced. . . .

PHIL

I don't believe you're serious.

JAMES

I'm a seasoned politician.

PHIL

You . . . against Sharmen.

JAMES

I can be mayor of this town.

PHIL

Half the time, more than half, it was your advice
that turned George into the village idiot.

JAMES

Phil, I kept his head above water. He suggested
stuffing the elephant and putting it in the museum.

PHIL

James, take a look at yourself. Take an honest look.
Sharmen attracts people, he's young . . . new . . .

he's poised. You're a school principal, and you also
work for the mayor, a patronage job. . . .
    (GEORGE *enters with basketball*)

GEORGE

He's putting on his girdle. Recognize this, huh?
    (He passes the ball suddenly to PHIL. PHIL
     throws it to TOM. TOM *to* JAMES. JAMES
       back to GEORGE*)*

TOM

Can't get the rhythm going without Martin.

GEORGE

But it's still there. All we need is some practice.
James, tell them my campaign slogan.

JAMES

Not now, George . . .

GEORGE

"Four more years of serenity and progress" . . .
    (Pause)
Don't you think it has a ring of security about it?

PHIL

If you have a choir of angels singing it.

GEORGE

It'll be expensive. We saturate the local stations with
it, billboards, etc., etc.

JAMES

Later, George, this is not the time . . .

GEORGE

We have a whole new image for me. A grass-roots
guy. Show me moving among the people. No egg-
head. Dynamic shots.

JAMES

George, will you please—

GEORGE

I'm dynamite on television.

JAMES

George, shut up a minute, will you!

GEORGE

What's the matter . . . something gone wrong here?

JAMES

Phil has serious doubts about us.

GEORGE

What?

JAMES

He doesn't think we can beat Sharmen.

GEORGE

Not after he hears a piece of very hot news we
picked up last week.

JAMES

What are you talking about?

GEORGE

My ace in the hole, James. Me and the coach kept it
even from you. A little research goes a long way, my
friends! Sharmen's uncle was a communist. *New
York Times*. June fifth. 1952. A blacklisted writer.
Hollywood.

PHIL

Old news. No one cares anymore. He's probably
dead.

GEORGE

He is!

PHIL

Can't hurt Sharmen.

GEORGE

In this town he is dead with a résumé like that!

JAMES

Are you sure, George? Are you absolutely positive,
not a shadow . . . ?

GEORGE

Uncontestable. The coach can give you more details.
Well, Phil, how do you stand now? There was a communist in his family!

PHIL

Times have changed. I can't depend on a hate vote.
Nobody knows or cares about his dead communist
uncle.

JAMES

It's a whole new ballgame, Phil.

PHIL

Ancient history.

JAMES

It's gotta hurt him.

PHIL

Wake up. It's 1972 already.

JAMES

(Dangerous)

George has taken good care of you, Phil. . . .

PHIL

I paid for it. My money got him elected last time.

JAMES

There's more to it than that and you know it.

PHIL

Is there?

JAMES

Yes, there is. See this suit? One hundred dollars.

Yours is silk, tailor made. Three hundred, huh? I
have a ten-year-old Ford and you get a new Cadil-
lac every year. Five kids. One a genius, maybe. I
support my alcoholic brother. Shut up! You're an
alcoholic, a marathon drunk. I am working my ass
off for George's victory because I want a share of
the spoils. I am a talented man being swallowed up
by anonymity! I want my share!

PHIL

You two guys fucked up. Share that!

JAMES

What's the next step, Phil, lunch with Sharmen?

PHIL

You sonofabitch.

GEORGE

James, calm down.

JAMES

Betrayal! It's nothing less than betrayal!

PHIL

Betrayal! Don't you mention betrayal to me.

JAMES

Listen to me, don't you understand what—

PHIL

Don't talk to me about betrayal, not after—

JAMES

Why are you so thick?

PHIL

Can I help it if you're nobody? . . .

JAMES

Pig-headed—

PHIL

Go on welfare!

JAMES

He's fucking your wife, George, that's why he won't support you.

GEORGE
(Pause)

Fucking who? What?

JAMES

Your wife, Marion.

GEORGE

When? Why?

PHIL

That is not why I won't support him.

GEORGE

Wait a minute. You're doing what with Marion?

PHIL

Georgie, we had a thing . . . it just happened.

GEORGE

Marion. Unfaithful. I'm the mayor, for Chrissakes!

PHIL

This was the wrong thing to do.

GEORGE

I need some . . . drink.
                    (Suddenly)
You should be dead! Wiped away like a dirty stain!

JAMES

George, my intention was not—

GEORGE

I know your intention.
                    (To PHIL*)*
You prey on people, you fucking animal.
                (Rips shotgun from wall)
Dead. You dirty dumb dago fucking animal bastard.
                (Points gun at PHIL*)*

COACH
                    (Enters)
Boys, here's the record. I hope I have a good needle.
Watch it, George, she's loaded.

GEORGE

I'm going to put Phil out of his misery!

COACH

What's the matter, what's happened, boys?

TOM

George, the safety is on.
(GEORGE *flicks the safety off*)

BLACKOUT

ACT TWO

*MEN are in exact positions that ended Act I.
Long pause. Gun trembles in GEORGE's hands.*

GEORGE

Fucking animal!

COACH

That's a hair trigger, a . . . it's loaded. I keep them
loaded.

GEORGE
(Whisper)

Dumb, dangerous animal.

JAMES

Why don't you put the gun down, George.

TOM

Yeah, we give up.

JAMES

You've got your career to think about. Killing Phil
is not worth it.

COACH
(Careful)

Don't lose your poise, boy, be a man and give me the

gun. It's all right . . . sit here . . . Okay. Easy,
boy.

(GEORGE *hands over the gun and begins to*
sob)

COACH
(*To* TOM)

Get him some Scotch . . . whisky. We'll work it
out, George, put our heads together.

GEORGE

I couldn't even shoot the fucking pig.

COACH

You've had too much to drink, can't hold it. You've
got a load, a tension in you, boy. Tense. Take deep
breaths, George, breathe deeply.

TOM

Maybe he should do some push-ups . . . run in
place.

(MEN *stare at him*)

COACH

Now, can you talk, George?

GEORGE
(*Weakly*)

Yes.

COACH

Fine. Now let's get to the bottom of this. What happened between you and Phil?

GEORGE

It's a private thing. . . .

COACH

Private? Nothing's private. There's been nothing private between the people in this room for twenty
years.
                    (Simultaneously)

JAMES

Phil is—

PHIL

Look, I—

GEORGE

It's my wife. I'll tell it.
                    (Gets up)
It's my story, right Phil, old pal . . . friend, great
guy . . . prick!

COACH

George!

GEORGE

I'm all right. Calm. Phil is having an affair with my
Marion.

COACH
(Pause)

Your Marion?

GEORGE

My Marion.

COACH

Continue, George.

GEORGE

I saved the man's business, put my political future on the line. I trusted my friend. You prick.

COACH

Get some air, George. Take him on the porch, James. . . . Is this true, Phil?

PHIL

It's over, Coach, you know, it just happened.

COACH

No, I don't know because I've never laid my friend's wife. What in Christ's name are you playin', boy, huh?

GEORGE
(*At window*)

He's nothing but a whore—

COACH

Enough now—

GEORGE

An old diseased whore!

COACH

I said, Enough!

(*To* PHIL)

You're pussy-whipped, boy, pussy-whipped! Get
some discipline. You think with your cock and it's
going to ruin you, boy, ruin you quicker than Sharmen, understand me? Somebody is going to scatter
you someday . . . all over the ground and, goddamit, there are people being hurt, people who have
their whole lives invested in this game you're playin'.
I'm stunned . . . shocked. I'm damn glad I have a
good heart 'cause this . . .

(*Sits*)

GEORGE

(*Yelling through window*)

Did she tell you you were the best, Phil, huh? Was
she good, tell your friends, you dumb dago. . . .

COACH

Get him in here. You'll announce it to the neighbor-
hood.

GEORGE

Sex maniac!

(*Enters*)

I want to know if my wife was a good lay.

COACH

What's wrong with you, it's none of your business!

GEORGE

What? . . .

COACH
(Pause)

What happened from beginning to end?

PHIL

She was there one day in my office, and—

COACH

When?

PHIL

Last month. She came to see me about campaign money.

GEORGE

She went to all the businessmen in town.

TOM
(Opening beer)

Wonder how much she raised.

JAMES

I'm warning you.

PHIL

We talked, had some drinks, it just happened. . . .

GEORGE

Right there in the office, for Chrissakes?

PHIL

It's a private office. . . .

COACH
(Pause)

On the floor?

PHIL

I have a couch in there. I asked her if she wanted to
uh . . . uh . . .

TOM

Fuck. The word is fuck.

PHIL
(To JAMES*)*

Shut that rummy up! And she said yes.

COACH

Just like that, like buying butter. Christ, Marion
never struck me as a whore.

GEORGE

Now wait a minute . . .

COACH

Jesus, you're really something. You're some dago.
Did you take her clothes off?

GEORGE

Now wait a minute . . .

COACH

I'm trying to establish who made the first advance.

PHIL

I don't remember, Coach.

TOM

This is better than *Rin Tin Tin Gets In*.

PHIL

We had a few drinks.

COACH

I see what you did. You doubled her drinks, got her hot on booze and memories, and humped her on the floor.

GEORGE

The couch, goddamit!

COACH

Enough said. You turn on each other, and you don't have a chance alone, not a solitary chance.

GEORGE

She's not a whore.

COACH

Nobody said she was. You need each other, boys, need—

GEORGE

I don't . . . need him.

COACH

I'm talking about survival. I'm talking about survival in the twentieth century.

GEORGE

I'm done with him.

COACH

You can't make it alone, George, not anymore. Gone forever, those days, gone.

GEORGE

You can't, after what's happened, expect me . . .

COACH

I didn't rot and die in the hospital . . .

GEORGE

. . . to even talk to . . .

COACH

. . . because I had you boys around me and . . .

GEORGE

Phil has betrayed everything and—

COACH
(Shouting)

I wasn't alone! I had you boys around me! They

didn't experiment with their needles on me, no sir, I
had you around me.

JAMES

George, the point he's trying to make—

GEORGE

I know the point, I know it, but it doesn't apply to
me, this situation.

COACH

I never could deal with ignorance, George, it dis-
gusts me!

GEORGE

He took advantage . . . of my wife. She hasn't
been the same since the baby, never got over it.
She resents me for putting it away. I wanted to
adopt a child, I told her, adopt right away.

COACH

You did the right thing. No man in this room faults
you, right?

JAMES
(Trying to sit GEORGE down)
Speaking for myself, I couldn't see any other way.

GEORGE
(Trying to come back)
I had chances to be unfaithful. The widows when

they cashed in the policy. I could have fucked fifty
widows. It was there! They wanted somebody to
keep them company.

COACH

Booze and women. I tried to protect you from it. I
got the Jesuits, got you scholarships, got the Jesuits
to teach you, boys. I graduated in three years from
the Jesuits. They all wanted me to become a Jesuit.
(Pause)
My father used to say the Jesuits were the scholars
of the Church.
(Pause)
But I liked my women . . . my booze . . . and
after a while I had my mother . . . I was all she
had.
(Pause)
Someday, I said, someday I'll marry. But time does
strange things. It's high tide before you know it, as
my father said, high tide.
(Pause)
Miss Morris, remember her, the music teacher?
(Slyly)
We knew each other for years. Biblically. Used to
visit her on Saturday afternoon. She'd make me
honey biscuits. A very cultured woman. Protestant.
Would never think of becoming a Catholic, my
mother was alive then, couldn't bring her here.
(Smiles)
She read poetry in French and wore silk stockings
and smoked cigarettes. Elegant. And she could

hump like a hundred-dollar whore and she loved
me on those Saturday afternoons. Fell dead in the
street seven years ago.

(Pause)

I never had the time. Teaching the game was not
just a profession, it was a vocation. Like a priest.
Devoted my life to excellence . . . superiority. So
don't come apart before my eyes, boys. Not in front
of me, because you, boys, are my real trophies,
never forget that, never.

JAMES

Every man in this room realizes that, Coach.

COACH

"Never take less than success."

JAMES

I still hear that in my sleep.

COACH

That's a philosophy of life, boys. Not a slogan, a
philosophy! We got a challenge comin' up. We beat
them by the rules, boys. Pride. Loyalty. Teamwork.
No other way.

TOM

(Mocking chant)

Beat the Jew, beat that Jew, beat that Jew—Gooo
Gentiles!

JAMES

You are ridiculous!

TOM

I'm absurd, are you kidding?

COACH
(Directly)

Why don't you take a walk, Tom.

TOM

I took one, remember?

COACH

But you came back.
(JAMES sits TOM on stairs)

PHIL
(Flatly)

I can't support George.

COACH

You will, Phil, after you hear some news. . . .

GEORGE

I told him already about Sharmen.

COACH
(Driving on)

Do you want to win this campaign, George?

GEORGE

I don't need him . . .

COACH

I didn't ask you that; I asked if you wanted to *win!*

GEORGE

Yes, I do but not—

COACH

Then you have to pay the price.

TOM

Who pays what? Huh? I mean, what price, what is
it?

COACH

Pain. The price is pain. You endure pain to win, a
law of life, no other way, none. The pain in my
gut. It's been there all my life. It's good to hurt. The
mind overcomes pain. You keep your marriage,
George. Hold onto it.
            (Pause)
We're waiting for your answer, Phil.

PHIL

I have to protect myself.

JAMES

You've already made a choice, haven't you?

COACH
(Unthinkable)

Not Phil, not my Phil.

(Hug)

Ya big moose, ya! I had to keep a bed check on you in high school, make sure you were in your own bed.

(Laughs)

PHIL
(Adamant)

Look, I'm sorry, but Sharmen's uncle could today be the head of the Red Army and he'd still beat George.

COACH

He was a commie.

PHIL

I don't even know if that's true!

COACH
(Pause)

When have I ever lied to you or you, anyone?

PHIL

No, I mean so what. . . .

COACH

FBI came to the school in the fifties. McCarthy was in his heyday then on television. They asked about

the uncle. Very casual. I knew what was up. I
didn't know the man, never saw him. They said
goodbye and that was that. I forgot all about it until
I was flat on my back in that hospital. We researched
it and discovered the whole truth!

PHIL

Why didn't you say something back in the fifties?

COACH

Why hurt a young boy? He wasn't a communist.

TOM

Why hurt him now?

COACH

He's on the other side now.

JAMES

He's opposition.

(Pause)

PHIL

I'm telling you, public opinion wants George back
in the insurance business.

JAMES

Public opinion is changed every day.

TOM
(Half-serious)

He's right, you know.

(Pause)

An hour listening to this and I'm ready to campaign for Sharmen.

COACH

I don't like that talk here, you . . .

JAMES

It's the liquor talking, Coach. Go to sleep, you're drunk.

TOM

I would but I think I pissed myself.

JAMES

Oh, Christ!

TOM

I think I should get up and go upstairs.

JAMES

Well, go up, for God's sake!

TOM
(Getting up)

Is it still in the same place?
(Looks down)
No. False alarm. I spilled my beer.

COACH

Don't let the booze beat you, boy. I'm behind you. Stand on your own two feet like the man you are.

GEORGE

Do you mind if I go up first? My stomach.

TOM

After you, Your Honor.
(Sits)

GEORGE
(On landing)
I expect that nothing will be settled without consult-
ing me.   *(Goes)*

JAMES

I want to say now, especially for Phil's benefit, that
what I did tonight was done, not for personal rea-
sons, but for the good of us all.

COACH

We all know that, James. Here, have a drink, Phil?

PHIL

Yeah.

JAMES

Let me explain myself. I felt only the truth would
bring us together again. I wouldn't hurt you inten-
tionally for the world, Phil.

PHIL

You don't have to convince me, James.

COACH
(Pause)
He took the Fifth Amendment eleven times.
(Pause)
A communist came through here, 1930 maybe. Bad
times. Poverty like a plague. Joyces across the
street ate their horse, gave some of it to my mother.
He came to organize. We broke his legs. Broke his
legs with a two-by-four and sent him packing.

PHIL
(Pause)
Things have changed today.

COACH
Nothing's different. Communists are at work today.
Worse! Students burning down colleges. They're
bringing a defeated army home, kill you in the
womb today, in the womb. Worse than the thirties.
Niggers shooting the police. Government gone bad.
And there's no McCarthy to protect us.

JAMES
He's out to get you, Phil.

COACH
Wants to ruin you, boy.

TOM
He's a Jew—that's good enough to beat him in this
town.

COACH

He's a smart Jewboy.

TOM

Why smear him with this communist thing?

COACH

Who's smearing? We are telling the truth. We win within the rules.

JAMES

He's not smearing Phil?

COACH
(To TOM directly)

Exploiting a man's weakness is the name of the game. He can't move to the left, you left him to death. Can't stop a hook, you hook away on him. Find his weak spot and go after it. Punish him with it. I drilled that into you a thousand times!

JAMES

My brother is accusing us of guilt by association!

TOM

Wrong. Guilt by accident. He can't choose his uncle.

COACH

You think that kike wouldn't use Marion against us? Wave her at us like a dirty flag?

TOM

Maybe he wouldn't.
>(GEORGE *comes down and stops at landing*)

JAMES

Listen, he took the Fifth Amendment—

TOM
(Flaring)

I've lived my life by taking the Fifth. So have you,
James.
>*(To himself)*

Everybody . . . along the line . . . sometime or
another.

JAMES

There was a communist in his family and that is all
we are interested in.

TOM
(Ruefully)

The Jesuits would be pissed at you, James.
>*(On stairs, deadpan)*

I expect that nothing will be settled without consult-
ing me.
>*(Goes)*

COACH

Breaks my heart to see him come apart like that,
a tragedy!
>*(Pause)*

It's up to you, Phil.

PHIL

I'm not convinced. I can't take a chance on him.
Can't you understand if I lose that business I'm
nothing? It's too late, there's nowhere to start over.

JAMES
(Holding phone)

Call him, Phil, right now.

PHIL

Who?

JAMES

Sharmen. You're planning to do it anyway.

PHIL

You're full of shit.

JAMES

Do it in front of us. Offer him a contribution. Call
953–8220.

PHIL
(Smiling)

How come you know his number?

JAMES
(Flustered)

Don't you try to insinuate against my loyalty. I
called him about a picture of a pig in a high school
newspaper! Oh forget it. He wouldn't take a contribution from you, anyway.

PHIL
(Taking phone, dialing)

Hello, Norman? This is the number one threat to the environment.

(Pause)

That's right, Phil Romano. The friendly pollutionist.

(Laughs)

It's all politics, right? Listen, I'll come right out with it and say I like your style. In fact, I'd like to talk over your campaign with you. What? Oh. Everybody needs some help. Money's tight, don't forget. I've been known to make a few political contributions now and then. What? No. No. You scratch my back and I scratch yours, it's that simple.

(Pause)

Is that so?

(Pause)

How's your uncle the communist, huh? You won't be laughing so hard when you read about it in the newspapers. You listen to me, you kike bastard, listen . . .

(Slams phone, enraged)

It was his cousin, not his uncle. Christ Almighty!

(Mutters in Italian)

COACH

It's still in the family, it's all right, we can still use it!

PHIL
(Accusing)

He laughed at me, fucking kike.

(To JAMES*)*

You made me blow it, James, you pushed me into blowing it!

JAMES

Phil, listen, if I wasn't your friend—

PHIL

Don't shit me. My money made my friends! Without my money, in school even, you wouldn't piss on me if I was on fire. My old man's money. Everybody got laid in the back seat of my car.

COACH
(Excited)

No goddam mockie is going to beat us on our home court! The crowd loves us.

PHIL
(Angry)

Politics is not basketball.

COACH

Hell, yes. You get the crowd behind you and you can't lose! Everybody votes for a winner, boys, you know that.

PHIL

We can't sit around fingering the Past. Nobody but us remembers that game for—

COACH

Cop stopped us tonight, took one look at me and ripped up the ticket.

(Elated)

He remembered that we gave this defeated town something to be proud of . . . a victory! We won the town that year.

PHIL

I'm no dummy and I know you can't fight progress. . . .

COACH

Progress? Nothing changes but the date.

GEORGE

Put a Jew in my place and you'll have progress all right.

COACH

Jews ruin a country. Nobody says it out loud but many think it, people never forget, they know.

JAMES

I think we should go easy on Sharmen being Jewish. It could be labeled anti-Semitism.

COACH

Yea Israel. I'm all for Israel. Give that one-eyed sonofabitch the seventh day and he would have blown those greasy Arabs off the face of the earth.

Arabs are communists. Wash their hair in camel piss. Let the Jews blow them the hell away. James, there're good and bad in every race. Nobody's anti-anything. Some of the greatest athletes in the world were Jews. Sid Luckman—magnificent! Nobody could punch like Barney Ross, pound for pound. Jesse Owens, alone, beat the goddam Germans, a splendid nigger, fast as the wind. But as a rule, watch them, can't trust them . . . Jews the same.

TOM
(Top of stairs)
My friends, I leave you with these words of wisdom. "In the kingdom of the blind . . ."
(He falls suddenly all the way down the steps.

MEN *rush to him)*

COACH
Don't move him. Broken bones.

JAMES
Tom, are you all right, Tom!

GEORGE
Maybe he's knocked out.

JAMES
Can you hear me, Tom?

COACH

Put him on the couch.

TOM

Somebody
                    (To GEORGE*)*
just fell down the steps over there.
                    (Sits)

TOM

James, this drinking in moderation is murder.

COACH

Get him a drink.

TOM

Get him a drink! ". . . the one-eyed man is king."
Before I was so rudely interrupted.

COACH
                    (Angry)
None of you can hold your liquor! Drink like
women. You'll be squatting to piss next.

PHIL

I want to talk to you alone, Coach.

COACH
                    (Getting drunk)
Uh-oh. Are you sober?

PHIL

Yeah.

COACH

Come out on the porch.
(They exit)

GEORGE

I don't trust Phil. Something's up.

JAMES

Let's let the coach handle it.

TOM

Why not? He's handled everything else. . . .

GEORGE
(To TOM*)*

We have nothing more to say to one another . . .
ever.

TOM

Fuck you and the horse you rode in on, as my old
grandmother used to say. Love you, George.
(Pause)
How's the little woman, huh?

JAMES

Shut up. Insensitive sonofabitch!
(The COACH *enters from porch. He silently
takes Fillmore H.S. sweater from the coat*

*rack and goes back to porch, closing door
behind him)*

GEORGE
(Pause)

You think I don't feel things, you think the old
clown doesn't have deep feelings, huh? Phony bullshit artist, huh? None of you know what goes on in
my head, nobody knows. I can understand . . .
understand what makes a man take a gun, go up a
tower, and start blowing people apart. I know the
feeling. All smiles, huh? I have rage in me . . . I
hate, hate like everybody, hate . . . things. I could
have taken his head off.

TOM

Why didn't you?

GEORGE

He wasn't worth it . . . I have a career to think
about.
(Pause)

In the hospital. Looked like something that floats
. . . in formaldehyde. Freakish. Blue eyes.

JAMES

This is not the time, George.

GEORGE
(Crying)

We put it away. Boy. Never even named it. Insti-
tutionalized it. Coach advised me . . . us, to give
it up. I pay four hundred a month.

JAMES

What else could you do?

GEORGE

A child like that . . . mongoloid . . . doesn't
help my career.

TOM

I need a beer.

GEORGE

It casts reflection . . . unfavorable to my image.
People get suspicious. . . . Advised me to put it
away immediately.

TOM

You lose the mongoloid vote, George, hands down
and—

JAMES

George, don't get drunk.
(High)
We have to make some important decisions tonight.

GEORGE

I can't get drunk enough. I don't need that bitch
either! We were going to renew our vows on our
fifteenth anniversary . . . on the altar. . . .

TOM

Why don't we stone her?

JAMES

Shut up.

TOM

There's an old Jewish custom, George.

GEORGE

Why are you doing this to me?

TOM

Stop leaking all over everybody. Stop the tragic act
and take the money. Stop this . . . dishonesty.

GEORGE

You always thought I was a phony, didn't you?

JAMES

Don't pay any attention. . . .

TOM
(To himself)

Unfuckingbelievable.

JAMES

George, . . .
(Commanding)
the coach is out there trying to convince Phil to
back us. Now I know he can do it. Question is—
will you accept the money from Phil? Now I think
we should consider . . .

TOM

Would you accept the money if it was Helen, your wife . . . ?

JAMES

Sonofabitch, I'm—

GEORGE

Yes, wait a minute, how about that question?

JAMES

I'm not in any such situation . . . it wouldn't apply.

GEORGE

Be me, James, imagine yourself me and a friend, boy you grew up with, champions, was fucking your wife. Imagine that awhile.

JAMES

It wouldn't happen.

GEORGE
(Shouting)

Pretend, just pretend you're me and answer me. Would you take the money?

JAMES
(Anger)

Yes, I'd take it, yes yes, take it all!

TOM

The Jesuits would really be pissed at you. . . .

JAMES

You're nothing but a . . . a complete and total disgrace. All cheap cynicism and booze.

TOM
(Warning)

Don't let's do my biography tonight, James.

JAMES

I saved your life, boy!

TOM
(Flaring)

You sound like him . . . "boy."

JAMES

Saved your life, and now I'm trying to save what's left of mine so stay out of it!

GEORGE
(Maudlin)

Stop it. Don't fight. Brothers should love . . . take care of each other.

JAMES

I carried him all my life, carried everybody. I'm exhausted at thirty-eight.

TOM

James never did anything out of . . . love. James never loved anything. He's just obedient. An obedient man. Press a button . . .

JAMES

No one's listening.

TOM

. . . and he shoulders a responsibility. But he can't sleep at night and his teeth fell out.

GEORGE
(Very maudlin)

I'm thirty-eight years old, used to have a thirty-two-inch waist, used to be the most popular boy in the school, used to have friends. Everything is in the past tense. I'm in the past tense.

JAMES

Your future is politics, George.

GEORGE

I can't find . . . myself. . . . I lose myself behind all the smiles, handshakes, speeches. I don't think I'm the man I wanted to be, I seem to myself to be somebody else. I'm always . . . can't stop watching myself. . . .

JAMES

It's all in the way you look at things. Your angle

of vision. Take Marion, for example. She may have
gone to Phil, did what she did, I'm not condoning
it, but she may have . . . with Phil, did the whole
thing for the money.

GEORGE

Why?

JAMES

Support you. Help you. It's entirely possible . . .
it's in the realm of possibility.

GEORGE
(Wanting to believe)

She was devoted to my career . . . I don't know,
maybe I don't even care.

JAMES

It's been done before.

GEORGE

She always said he couldn't be trusted, use the
stupid slob, you may be right, James.

JAMES

She probably recognized the problem before we did.

GEORGE

I wouldn't put it past her, you could be right, yes,
you could.

TOM

I think she just humped him out of plain old lust,
George.

GEORGE
(Bravado)
I'll see you when I'm sober for that remark!

TOM

You're up for sale tonight, George, going cheap tonight.

JAMES

See what he does to me, me who went to another
city to find him. He called and I went to another
city to find him. How many times? How many cities?
You were nothing but rags! Filth. I picked you up,
carried you screaming into a hospital.

TOM

Nobody held a gun. . . .

JAMES

I had no choice!

TOM

Only alkies like me have no alternatives, James.

JAMES

Do you know what the old man left me? He left me
when he finally died six thousand in medical bills

and twelve hundred for the funeral. And me, old faithful, ends up ten years behind everyone else and for what?

GEORGE

We all have great respect for you, James, you sacrificed, well, you know.

JAMES

Mediocrity. My son, Jimmy, the bright one, asked me what it meant, definition of the word mediocrity. "It means of low excellence." You know why he asked? Because that's what he thinks of me, how he sees me, how I'm beginning to see myself.

GEORGE

The school super job is all yours after the elections.

JAMES

That's only the beginning. I found my talent late in life. I didn't get into politics until I was over thirty. There's always Congress, George, Congress in the distance. I'm going to make my stand in the political arena.

(PHIL *comes in, shirt open*)

PHIL

He wants to talk to you, George.

GEORGE

Me?

PHIL

Yeah.

GEORGE

No.

PHIL

He's waiting.
                    (Pause)
            (GEORGE *fixes tie, exits to porch)*

TOM
            (Pause)
The suspense is killing.

PHIL

Like before a game. Drink?

TOM

Thank you.

JAMES

George will accept the money, Phil.

PHIL

Good. Ice?

TOM

No.

JAMES

How are you disposed?

PHIL

You mean how do I feel about it? Iffy. It's all iffy.

JAMES

What's the Coach say?

PHIL

We got a town of dress factories, right, car lots, bars and empty mines, and some Jew thinks he's going to turn it into Miami Beach.

JAMES

He's going to try. But if we can coordinate our-selves—

PHIL

Who cares? Do I really care? I'm so bored half the time it's killing me. Watching the same old faces get old, same bullshit, day in and day out. Bored. Some-times I get on the turnpike and just drive until I feel like getting off. Alone. I ended up in Binghamton last week. One hundred miles on a Friday night by myself. Believe that! What's left? Hit a few bars, some music, drink, play old basketball games over in my head. Pick up some strange pussy now and then, here and there, you know. Always need some-thing young and juicy sitting beside me. Mostly sit and replay the good games in my head, believe that?

JAMES

We were good.

PHIL

Could call each other's moves . . . every time.

JAMES

We had some good times, great.

PHIL

Sometimes I think that's the only thing I can still feel, you know, still feel in my gut, still feel that championship season, feel the crowds . . . my best memory to date, yeah, nothing matched it, nothing.

JAMES
(Warmly)

We were good then.

TOM

Martin.

PHIL

Think about him all the time too.
(Pause)
I loved that guy.

JAMES

The perfect ballplayer, wasn't he?

PHIL

Yeah. Know what I do for excitement now?

TOM

We all have a good idea!

PHIL

No, no. Everybody does that. I got a Porsche now.
Fuel injector, water pump. James Dean, right?
Upped it to one twenty coming back from Binghamton. Smashed. Everything a blur. Can't see the road
but I'm laughing my ass off, laughing so hard I have
to wipe my eyes and now I'm hitting one thirty-five
and have only one hand on the wheel, pissed out of
my mind, radio blaring and suddenly, it's crazy, but
I think I'm just speed and I know nothing can catch
me, nothing alive can touch me and I open her up to
one forty. Shit-scared. And everything becomes a
blur but I'm laughing because I know nothing on
earth can catch me.

(Pause)

Some Friday night they'll be putting pieces of me
in a rubber bag.

(Pause)

Wonder what it's like to get it at one hundred forty
miles an hour.

TOM

Splat.

PHIL

Yeah. Like a bug hitting the windshield.

JAMES

Sounds more dangerous than married women.

PHIL

(Laughs)

James is offended by—

JAMES

No, no, it was a joke.

PHIL

Offended. Know why I like married women? Nobody gets involved. They don't yell, tell, swell, and
they're grateful as hell. Marion took my cherry in
school . . . nobody gets involved . . . I really
cared for her. She's a bitch now, a bitch on wheels,
he did a job on her, she's finished. I thought maybe
we could go back to something, see if it was still
there . . . it ain't like the movies, she's a bitch now.

JAMES

I don't understand women like her, never did, never
wanted to.

PHIL

Better watch your Helen.

JAMES

My Helen. Never happen. Helen does everything by
the book. No, Helen is a champion of chastity. Sex
is children, children is sex. She'd be happy spending
the rest of her life putting cocoa butter on her tits
. . . breasts. She's only happy when she's pregnant.
Clears up her skin.

PHIL

She still paint?

JAMES

Not really.

PHIL

She won all the art prizes. She was the only one that
didn't laugh at me that time. Remember? In art
class, we had to identify paintings for the exam
and I said mine was an El Gresso and you laughed
out loud and somebody else laughed behind me and
soon the whole class was laughing, even me, but I
remember she didn't . . . laugh. . . .
                    (Pause)

JAMES

You smell something?

PHIL

What? The chicken!
                    *(*JAMES *into kitchen)*
Burned bad?

JAMES

No. Hot. I'll bring it out.

TOM

Did old Marion laugh?

PHIL

Don't worry about George. He'll get over it.

TOM

Think so, huh?

PHIL

You could rub the two of them together and you

wouldn't get a sound. All this shit about her being
ripped up about the baby.

TOM

She didn't want it?

PHIL

No. She had to convince him! He wanted to keep
it. Wouldn't give it up until the coach damn near
ordered him to. Hey, I'm not the first guy she laid,
she's been running around the last few years.

TOM

Why doesn't she leave him?

PHIL

Where's she going at thirty-eight?
            (Pause)
You're an alcoholic.

TOM

What ever gave you that idea?

PHIL

Jesus Christ . . . what happened?
            (Pause)
Do you need any money?

TOM

I'll let you know.

PHIL

Sharmen's got class, style. George is like Bugs Bunny on television. "This is the mayor. What's up, folks?" We got Looney Tunes for a mayor.

(JAMES *enters with chicken, then runs upstairs*)

(*To* TOM)

George isn't a modern man. It's that simple. I am; maybe you, too. You know, Claire and me, we have an arrangement.

(*Pause*)

It's civilized. Nothing lasts forever. As long as she doesn't make it with anyone in the town, none of my friends, fine, you know, it's a mutual arrangement. You have to change with the times . . . be modern.

(*Pause*)

Don't say anything to the rest, between me and you.

TOM

(*To himself*)

I think I'm medieval, yeah, probably somewhere in the Dark Ages.

PHIL

Yeah, she and her old lady fly all over. She's never home. On my money. The old lady knows she makes it with other men. Isn't that something, believe that, they talk about it . . . I wonder if it's a crime in this state to fuck your mother-in-law.

TOM

Ask Brother James. He's the keeper of perversions.
Hey James!

PHIL

I'm going to get a vasectomy.

TOM

Is that so?

(JAMES enters)

PHIL

They tie up your tubes. You come but you don't
come sperm. Sterilized.

(Pause)

I fuck a lot, you know, and I can't afford any more
abortions. And two kids is enough. I told Claire,
we discussed it and . . . she agrees . . . it's the
intelligent thing to do.

(Pause)

You're right, everybody around here lives in the
Dark Ages, pitch black.

(GEORGE enters)

GEORGE

He wants to talk to you, James.

(JAMES exits front door)

TOM

George, have some chicken.

(Long pause)

(COACH *and* JAMES *enter*)

JAMES

You want me to step down as your campaign manager.

GEORGE

Phil has contacted these—

JAMES

You dump me now and my politics are over.

GEORGE

James, Phil has contacted these advertising people in Philadelphia.

JAMES

People will know I've been dumped. I wouldn't be able to buy a vote. You'd ruin me in this town.

GEORGE

After the election I can still endorse you for superintendent.

JAMES

After dumping me from running your campaign.

COACH

James, we need a very experienced man in that position. We are just bringing in some professional help. You'll still be involved in the campaign.

JAMES
(To PHIL)
You did this, you've turned them against me.

PHIL
James. I can't put twenty-five thousand, thirty, in the hands of an amateur.

JAMES
I am not going to take this lying down. Spoiled ignorant lout is not going—

PHIL
It's not what you think.

JAMES
You're an ignoramus!

PHIL
You're a shabby man.

JAMES
And you're a goddam ignoramus!
　　(PHIL *slaps* JAMES *across the face. A dental
　　　　plate falls from* JAMES's *mouth)*
My teeth . . .
　　　　(On knees)
You've broken my teeth. I'll kill you . . . ignorant . . .
　　　　(Near impotent rage)

TOM
(Picks it up)
It's not broken. Go on upstairs.
(Pause. To PHIL*)*
If I had my wits, some anger, some guts, I'd take
your head off, Phil.

PHIL
I'm just money to you guys! I'm money to everybody! I'm not giving it away, no more charity from
the dumb dago!

JAMES
(Controlled)
If you people do this to me I will walk every street
in this town, hear me, and tell every single person
about Phil and Marion.

PHIL
Shabby.

JAMES
I will not be abused like this. I will turn George into
the village idiot.

GEORGE
You wouldn't do that, James.

JAMES
I swear it by Christ, and your brother-in-law, and the
kickbacks on the city's jobs.

GEORGE

You'd ruin me. . . . You'd ruin us. . . .

JAMES

What did you just do to me?

PHIL

An hour ago he suggested that we back him for mayor.

COACH

I don't believe that.

PHIL

Ask him.

JAMES

I proposed an alternative!

GEORGE

I'm sick . . . help me . . , my stomach is upset.

COACH

Can you make it upstairs?

GEORGE

I think so.
> *(Suddenly he lunges toward trophy)*

COACH

Not in the trophy.

BLACKOUT

ACT THREE

MEN *are in exact positions that ended Act II.*

TOM

Nice shot, George.

COACH

I'll take him upstairs. Clean him up.

GEORGE

I can't get my breath. . . .

COACH

Then stop talking.
(On landing with GEORGE)
Wash out the trophy, James. Under cold water.
(JAMES exits to kitchen with trophy)

TOM

Dull night, maybe I should go and fall down the stairs again. . . .

PHIL

It gets more desperate, people get more desperate.
(Yelling)
Why is everyone so fucking desperate? Everyone wants a piece of me. Like Namath, right? I'm only my money . . . nothing else.
(Takes out paper)

This is a dentist's bill. Four thousand dollars. My
wife. For four thousand dollars you could cap a
shark's mouth. I'm expected to finance everybody's
life.

(Pause)

Marion brought up the campaign money. About the
third time I laid her, she brought it up, very casually,
and then talked about it for three hours.

(Pause)

I expected it . . . I knew it . . . she laid it in.
Well, she worked for it! I made her earn it!

TOM

You wanted George to . . . find out.

PHIL

Yeah. Maybe. I don't know, she worked for it. I took
her up to the Holiday one afternoon and fucked her
on the bed, floor, chair, tub, toilet . . . everywhere
but the ice machine.

(Pause)

You know the only woman I ever loved . . . my
mother, fuck the psychiatrists . . . my mother is
the only . . . woman I ever knew. The rest are all
cunts.

TOM

I don't care, you know. The truth is I don't care
about the melodrama of your life.

(JAMES enters)

JAMES
(Pause)
I have been betrayed by my friends.
(No response)
I carried that imbecile Polack four years, him and
his nymphomaniac wife.

PHIL
Watch it.

JAMES
I know, I was his best man. The ushers were com-
paring notes on her. George got sick before the
wedding too. Threw up with joy.

PHIL
We know her past history, James. No lectures . . .

JAMES
You don't know anything. You fornicated and read
the newspapers. That's what you know. But nobody
is going to abuse me, use me, nobody.

TOM
"Now we won't have James to kick around anymore."

JAMES
Exactly. I'm a new man. And I come high. My success has been delayed by my responsibilities, my
youth was given over to my responsibilities and now

it is my turn, and now I am going to demand my right to success . . . demand. I had, Christ I'm ashamed, to borrow the money from Phil to bury him.

PHIL

You don't owe me anything.

JAMES

I owe. Everybody. I don't own a goddam thing.

PHIL

I won big on the Colts.

JAMES

And now you knife me in the back.

PHIL

James, I like being rich, okay. I need money. I want two of everything. Cars, boats, women, etc., etc. Around expensive things I get a hard on, turned on, I want them. My old man was like you, James, desperate. He built a business twenty-four hours a day, didn't have time to learn the language, two words he knew, money and work; no, three, the business. The business killed him at forty-fucking-three and we buried a man nobody ever knew. I worked for my old man, slept with him, ate, and I have no memory of who he was, what he was. The fucking business is mine now.

(Pause)

It's all mine.

(COACH *enters*)

COACH

He's cleaned up. Going to call his wife. I'm bewildered.

(Pause)

Stunned. Never. Knocked on my ass! Never did I think I'd live to see you turn savagely . . . savagely turn on each other. You're not the same people who played for me.

TOM
(Drunkenly to himself)

We are a myth.

COACH

What?

TOM

Myths!

COACH

Is that trophy a myth! See the names engraved on it! Don't grow old on me, boys, don't lose faith, don't get old on me. I carved your names in silver, last forever, forever, never forget that, never. Nothing changes but the date, boys. You're all still immensely talented. . . .

JAMES

I'm a junior high school principal who has to have
the walls scrubbed every day because inevitably
some little bastard scribbles all over them, "Mr.
Daley eats it . . . Daley is a shit head."

COACH

Taking care of your father slowed you up. . . .

JAMES
(Pause)
Slowed me up. I wiped the man's ass, like a baby,
rubbed his body with oil, washed him, I had to feed
him before he died and in all those years I never felt
. . . love from him. He'd get drunk and abuse me.

COACH

In fever, bedridden, a man can say strange things.

JAMES

I just want . . .

COACH

What?

JAMES

I want . . . wanted . . .

COACH

What!

JAMES

I wanted him to respect me . . . respect me, that's all I wanted.

COACH

Whine! You're a thirty-eight-year-old whine! Bitch and whine and blame your life on everybody. You got the eyes of a beggar. . . . Did they respect me? Thirty years a teacher . . . a coach, a teacher devoted to excellence. Did they respect me when they forced me into retirement? Gave me a farewell dinner, gold watch, and a pension. A pension is a ticket to death, a goddam passport. Said I was old-fashioned, said I abused a student . . . the boy made an obscene gesture to my face and I hit him—what's old-fashioned about that?

JAMES

You broke his jaw. . . .

COACH

And the next thing I know I'm walking the streets at eight o'clock in the morning with nowhere to go . . . start listening to the radio . . .
            (To himself)
I watch more T.V. than any man alive. You make them respect you.
            (George enters)

GEORGE
            (Pause)
I talked to Marion.

(*To* JAMES)

You were right. Absolutely.

JAMES
(*Weary*)

Was I?

COACH

What did she say?

GEORGE

She did it for me, for the money.

COACH

You heard that, Phil.

PHIL

I know.

TOM

Next time, the ice machine, right, Phil?

GEORGE

It's late. I better leave now. . . .

TOM

She convince you to take the money, George?

GEORGE

That's none of your goddam business.

TOM

After old James gets through, they're going to give
you a pair of horns on the steps of city hall.

COACH

That is not going to happen.

JAMES

I mean what I said.

GEORGE

Marion said the whole—

COACH
(Sharply)

I don't care what that hot-pantsed bitch said. Go
home and kick her ass all over the kitchen. All that
slutting around—

GEORGE

She's not a slut—

COACH

She was punished for slutting, wasn't she? She was
punished and so were you!

GEORGE

That's a terrible thing to say.

COACH

Leave her the hell out of the campaign . . . lock
her in her room . . . she's trouble, she is.

GEORGE
(Quietly)

You know I have pride in—

COACH

You have no pride, none. You got a face for everybody. All slick smiles and empty eyes. You lost
something, boy, lost something. . . .
(Pacing)
Phil playin' the lout screwing and ruining his life
away. Lost something.
(To TOM)
You stumbling and reeling through the streets like
some broken thing, hearing people laugh at you,
breaks my . . . you were a gifted boy. . . .

TOM

Past tense.

COACH

Gifted! Unbelievable talent. Not just basketball. All
of you. I remember James, remember sitting in that
auditorium watching James win, what contest was it,
what?

JAMES

I speak for democracy. . . .

COACH

I speak for democracy. You held that audience spellbound. When you stood up to speak the whole crowd

hushed, no movement, still. They were spellbound. You overwhelmed them. I'll never forget it.

JAMES

I won a hundred-dollar bond. . . .
> *(Rueful)*

The old man cashed it in and drank it up.
> *(Pause)*

TOM

Yeah . . . gave you a little gold cup.

COACH

"Run to win." St. Paul said that, a saint, run always to win. I drilled that into you. "Healthy minds, healthy bodies," Greeks said that, boys, and they started it all, great athletes, the Greeks, magnificent!

TOM

Greeks were pederasts.

COACH

What the hell is he talking about?

JAMES

He means the Greeks were homosexuals.

COACH
> *(Shocked)*

The Greeks homos? Not the Greeks, the Romans, maybe, but not the Greeks! Don't come around me

with that liberal bullshit. I won't listen. The Greeks
made their men into gods.

      (Pause. Recites with deep conviction)

The credit belongs to the man who is actually
    in the arena,
Whose face is marred by dust and sweat and
    blood.
A man who knows the great enthusiasms and
    the great devotions.
Who spends himself in a worthy cause. . . .
Who in the end knows the triumph of high
    achievement
And if he fails, at least fails while daring greatly
So that his place shall never be with those cold
    and timid souls
Who know neither victory nor defeat.

That's a man's words. A man among men. Monday
morning, boys, we start on Sharmawitz, we get into
the arena and draw some blood.

                  JAMES
              (Not taken in)
Not James, not me, not till my participation is settled.

                  COACH
It's been settled!

                  JAMES
Not to my satisfaction.

COACH
(Pause)

Phil, as soon as possible, contact those people in Philadelphia.

PHIL

Okay.

JAMES

You will not change your minds?

COACH

Get them up here by Monday.

JAMES

No one is going to walk over me. I'm done. My back's against the wall. I will walk the streets of this town . . . I will . . . do you hear me ? . . .

GEORGE

James.

JAMES

Who the hell are you? I don't know you. I'm going out there and open up . . . I will . . .
(Sits; pause)

Low excellence.

TOM

Welcome to anonymity, James.

(*To* COACH)

No bench. No depth. Playing with too many injuries.

COACH

You've been sneering at us all night. Laughing in our faces.

TOM

Don't start on me. I'm not here. I'm in New Orleans.

COACH

You're finished. Useless. And you had talent. You quit on everyone who needed you. . . .

TOM

Stop lying to us. Stop telling us how good we were.

COACH
(*To* TOM)

We never had a losing season and we're not starting now. . . .

TOM

That's not what Martin said.

COACH

What?

TOM

Martin? Remember him?

COACH

Yeah.

TOM

But he's not here. You know why he left, why he never came back to a reunion.

COACH
(Pause)

Do I?

TOM

He told us the truth, twenty years ago.

COACH

Did he?

TOM

He wanted you to publicly refuse the trophy, remember? You told him in the third quarter to get that nigger center, the kangaroo, remember? He did. He went out and broke the guy's ribs.

COACH

I told him to stop him. That nigger was playing him off the court, and I told him to get tough under the boards and stop him.

TOM

He came to you a week after the game.

COACH

That's right, he did. He came to me . . . he walked in here. He came babbling something about the truth. What truth, I said, we won. That trophy is the truth, the only truth. I told him to get mean, punish some people, put some fear into them, you have to hate to win, it takes hate to win. I didn't tell him to break anybody's ribs.

(Pause)

You don't believe me, boys?

(Appeal to majority)

GEORGE

I believe you, Coach.

TOM

We have gone through this phony ritual, champions? Shit! We stole it.

COACH

I told him there is no such thing as second place.

TOM

Never less than success. Pay the price. Get yourself a name. I did. I really did. I fell on my ass in ten cities, that's a record.

(Takes whiskey)

Here's my trophy.

COACH

I read the fine print on you.

TOM

Find the other man's weakness—exploit him—hook him to death.

(Manic)

Watch out—they're out to get you. . . .
(Laughs)
Get that sonofabitch before he gets you, win, win,
only sin is losing, bless me Father for I . . . Christ,
I'm sick.

COACH

Need to lose.

TOM

Look it in the eye, old man, we stole that trophy,
championship season is a lie. Say that out loud . . .

COACH
(Putting trophy in TOM's *hands)*
Deny that. You can feel it. It has weight. Deny it.
Read the names in silver there.

TOM
(Anguish)
I don't believe in trophies anymore! . . .
(COACH *slaps him across the face)*

(Pause)
. . . empty.

COACH

Get out.

TOM

And Martin?

COACH

Out.

TOM

I got a ticket somewhere.

(Exits)

GEORGE

Coach, Martin tried to tell me the same story.

PHIL

Martin was a real sonofabitch when you think about it.

JAMES

Martin didn't have a brain in his head.

COACH

We don't need them, boys. . . . It's history now. In the books. You were a rare and a beautiful thing, boys . . . a miracle to see people play beautifully together . . . like when I was a boy . . . long time past . . . the whole town would come together. We'd have these huge picnics, great feasts of picnics. My father ran the only bank in town. An elegant man. Bach was played in this house. He quoted Shakespeare, "To be or not to be, that's the question." Shoulders like a king . . . he carried me on his back into the freezing, God, yes, waters of the lake. So clear you could see the white pebbles on the bottom. Gone now, all gone, vanished. Lake, picnic grounds, gone now. All concrete and wires and glass now. Used-car lots now. Phil's trucks came and took it away.

GEORGE

We can bring it back, Coach, urban renewal, preserve the environment.

COACH

Jesus, I can still see buckets of ice cream . . . great red slabs of beef . . . kites, yes, the sky full of blue and red kites, men playing horseshoes, big silver pails of beer, in the late afternoon the men would dive from the high rocks, so high they made you dizzy to look down. I watched my father dive and turn and glisten in the sun, falling like a bird falls, and knife the water so clean as to leave only ripples. The Depression killed him. The bank went under. His hair turned white. He threw his wedding ring away, threw his teeth across the room, stopped talking. He died a year later in his prime. Wouldn't let anybody in the room, not even my mother, died alone in the room. He lost faith in everything, the country. He told me, that man who listened to Bach, quoted Shakespeare, elegant man, he told me, "Never forget Marx was a Jew, Jews will ruin the country." Twenty-nine killed him dead.

(Sudden rage)

Not enough of them jumped out of windows in twenty-nine, the whole race should have splattered on the sidewalks in twenty-nine. The man didn't know how to fight back. He lost his character. Lost his character.

(Pause)

I chose my country, God forgive me. I made the supreme sacrifice and went to work in the mines for my country. You got to fight back, fight back, fight forever! They killed McCarthy too. Kennedy. Patton, even.

(Pause)

There are no leaders, boys, all the great ones in stone. Somebody has to lead the country back again. I'm talking about survival. All we have is ourselves, boys, and the race is to the quickest and this country is fighting for her life, and we are the heart and we play always to win!

(Drunk but in control)

You won't lose, boys—because I won't let you lose, I'll whip your ass to the bone, drive you into the ground. Your soul belongs to God but your ass belongs to me, remember that one, yes sir, we can do it, we are going to win because we can't lose, dare not lose, won't lose, lose is not in our vocabulary! I shaped you boys, never forget that. I ran you till the blisters busted, ran you right into perfection, bloody socks and all; you had no character, you couldn't put on your jocks, awkward, all legs, afraid, a mistake a second. I made you winners. I made you winners.

(COACH *puts on the record*)

(During the playing of the record, the MEN *sit, transfixed by the memory. No movement)*

RECORD
(Harsh, cracked tones)

Ten seconds left. Fillmore High School has fought
their way back from a near disastrous first half. They
are behind now by one point, seventy-one to seventy.
But they have the ball with ten seconds on the clock.
George Sikowski will throw the ball to either Tom
Daley or Martin Roads. Ten seconds. Pennsylvania
State Basketball Championship game comes down to
one shot, one play. Here we go, time in. Sikowski
passes to Daley, Daley in the back court. A pass to
James Daley in the corner, Daley across court to
Romano. Five seconds! Romano to Daley, Daley
to Roads at the foul line. Two seconds! Roads up
and shoots! Yes, yes! Fillmore High School wins it!

(Loud crowd noise, then silence. TOM *enters
—goes to the* COACH. *Then sits.* GEORGE
*drunkenly starts the school song. The others
join in)*

GEORGE AND OTHERS

Another victory for Fillmore
As we swing into the fray
For the loyal sons of Fillmore are out to win
     today,
With hope and courage never failing
As we swing right down the field
Our hearts will e'er be faithful
To the foe we'll never yield.

(Suddenly PHIL *starts to sob)*

COACH
(Goes to PHIL)

Don't punish yourselves, boys, the world will do that, protect . . . survive.

(Pause)

Phil, do you have something to say to George?

PHIL
(Goes to him)

I'm sorry. Forgive me. Sorry.

(They hug and cry)

(Pause)

TOM
(Quietly)

Whoop! whoop. Whooping cranes, us and the whooping cranes . . .

COACH

Wha's that?

TOM

On the way out. Cranes. Whoop.

COACH

Love one another, boys. No way a man can do it alone. Got to belong to something more than yourself.

JAMES

George, I'll do anything you want, I'm behind you.

GEORGE

You dirty bastard, I love you like a brother.

COACH
(With camera)

All right, album time.
(The men gather around the trophy)

GEORGE

We better get together and start mapping it all out.

COACH

Monday at twelve. The mayor's office. You need a speech for the K of C next Thursday.

GEORGE

James?

JAMES

We'll have it to you by Monday.
(MEN *gather around trophy)*

COACH

Smile. Let's see them new teeth, James.
(Takes their picture)

(Pause)

JAMES

Let's have one of you, Coach.

COACH

No. Not me, not me, not me.

GEORGE

One for the album, Coach.
> (COACH *goes to the trophy. Holds it in his
> arms and poses for the picture*)

PHIL

Why don't you come over tomorrow and watch the
playoffs in color?

COACH

No. The game's changed. The good little man is ex-
tinct. I hardly watch it anymore. They all shoot
down at the basket now. I hardly watch it anymore.
Not my game. It's no longer the white man's game.

GEORGE

C'mon, smile, Coach.

TOM

Say cunnilingus.
> (*The lights on stage fade out, leaving only a
> spot on the* COACH. *The flash of the camera*)

JAMES

I got you, Coach.

COACH

Yeah.

FADEOUT

JASON MILLER

Jason Miller was born in 1939 and grew up in Scranton, Pennsylvania. After studying at the University of Scranton and Catholic University, he has pursued the dual career of actor and playwright, appearing in *Long Day's Journey into Night* with Helen Hayes, *Juno and the Paycock* with Geraldine Fitzgerald, and as Rogozhin in *Subject to Fits* at the Public Theater. He is the author of three one-act plays and *Nobody Hears a Broken Drum,* which was produced off-Broadway in 1970. Mr. Miller lives in New York City with his wife and three children.